WHERE DOES RUBBISH GO?

Sophy Tahta

Designed by Lindy Dark
Illustrated by Colin King and Guy Smith
Edited by Cheryl Evans
With thanks to Friends of the Earth

CONTENTS

Consultant checker: Chris Murphy

All sorts of rubbish

You probably throw things away when they are old or broken or when you just don't want them anymore.

But your rubbish is only a tiny part of the mountains of waste thrown out each year all over the world.

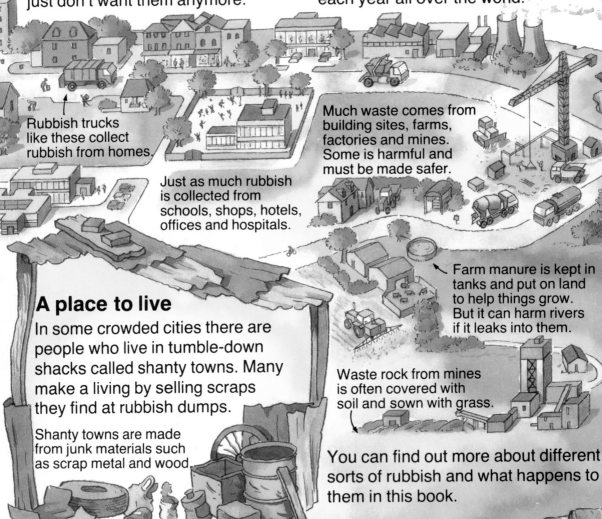

Rubbish trucks like these collect rubbish from homes.

Just as much rubbish is collected from schools, shops, hotels, offices and hospitals.

Much waste comes from building sites, farms, factories and mines. Some is harmful and must be made safer.

Farm manure is kept in tanks and put on land to help things grow. But it can harm rivers if it leaks into them.

A place to live

In some crowded cities there are people who live in tumble-down shacks called shanty towns. Many make a living by selling scraps they find at rubbish dumps.

Shanty towns are made from junk materials such as scrap metal and wood.

Waste rock from mines is often covered with soil and sown with grass.

You can find out more about different sorts of rubbish and what happens to them in this book.

2

Space junk

Millions of parts of spacecraft have been left in space. These could damage new ones going there. People need to clear up this junk, too.

Rubbish in the wrong place

Litter is rubbish that is dropped on the ground, into rivers or in the sea.

Ships throw tons of old nets and plastic rubbish in the sea each day, even though this is not allowed.

Sea litter can trap and choke turtles, seabirds, whales, fish and seals.

Broken glass and sharp cans left on the ground can cut animals.

Clues to the past

People called archaeologists study the things which others once threw away or left behind, to find out more about how they used to live.

Some of the things archaeologists dig up are thousands of years old.

You can help to stop litter from hurting animals or spoiling the view by putting yours in bins.

Not everything you throw away is rubbish. Notice the sorts of things you throw away each week. Most can be used again, as you will see.

3

Clearing up

Rubbish from shops, homes, schools, and so on is put into all sorts of bins or bags. These are collected and emptied into rubbish trucks which crush the rubbish to pack more in.

Places such as schools or shops put rubbish in big, plastic or metal bins with wheels. Some homes do too.

Rubbish trucks carry rubbish from hundreds of bins and bags.

This truck is filled up and emptied several times a day.

This is called a packer blade. It slides down, scoops rubbish into the truck and squeezes it against a panel.

Lots of trucks are fitted with special lifts. These lift up and tip out bins of all sizes.

Bin lids keep smells and rubbish in and animals out.

This powerful machinery could be dangerous if you get too near.

As more rubbish is crammed in, this panel slides back to make more room.

Rubbish must be collected often or it can start to rot and attract rats and flies which spread diseases.

4

Cleaning the street

All sorts of machines are used to clean roads. In some places a street cleaner also sweeps pavements and empties litter bins into a cart.

This hose can be pulled out to suck up dead leaves and litter.

This pipe sucks rubbish into the truck through a wide nozzle.

Nozzle

Strong brushes wash and scrub the road.

Water is sprayed out of holes in the nozzle and brushes.

People who collect rubbish and clean streets start early when roads are clear. Some even work at night.

Special collection

Venice in Italy has canals for streets. Rubbish is collected there by barges.

In cities such as Paris in France, special scooters suck dog mess into a box with a hose.

Everest is the highest mountain in the world.

So much litter has been left on Mount Everest, that a team of climbers has been to pick it up.

5

On the move

In many towns, rubbish trucks dump their rubbish at a place called a transfer station. From here it goes to big holes in the ground called landfills.

Tipped out

At some transfer stations, rubbish is tipped straight into a machine called a compactor.

This back end lifts up.

Rubbish trucks are too slow and heavy to go far. They will only go straight to a landfill if there is one near enough.

This panel slides forward, pushing rubbish out.

The rubbish falls down a chute called a hopper.

Box

Boxed in

A huge metal bar at one end of the compactor shoves rubbish into a long metal box clamped to the other end.

Rubbish from four trucks is pressed or compacted into one box. This saves space.

Compacter ram

This bar is called a ram. It slides to and fro under the hopper.

Full boxes slide away from the compactor on metal rails, so that this door can be shut.

6

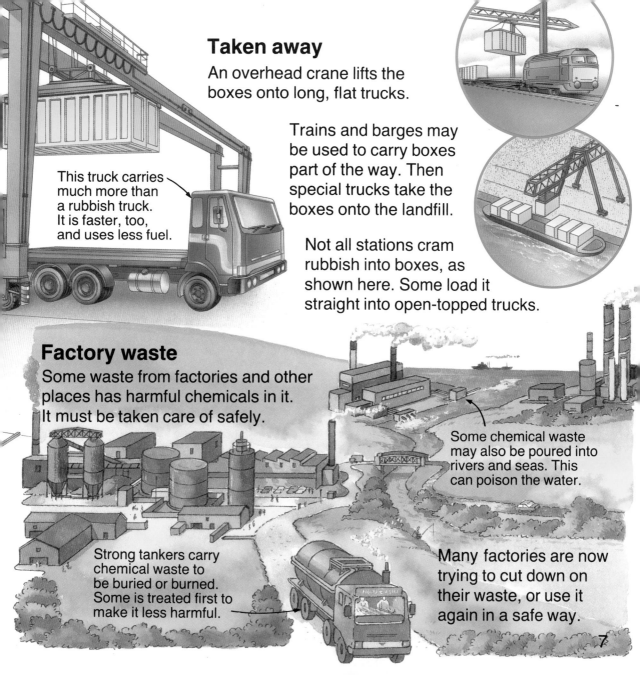

Taken away

An overhead crane lifts the boxes onto long, flat trucks.

This truck carries much more than a rubbish truck. It is faster, too, and uses less fuel.

Trains and barges may be used to carry boxes part of the way. Then special trucks take the boxes onto the landfill.

Not all stations cram rubbish into boxes, as shown here. Some load it straight into open-topped trucks.

Factory waste

Some waste from factories and other places has harmful chemicals in it. It must be taken care of safely.

Some chemical waste may also be poured into rivers and seas. This can poison the water.

Strong tankers carry chemical waste to be buried or burned. Some is treated first to make it less harmful.

Many factories are now trying to cut down on their waste, or use it again in a safe way.

7

Rotting away

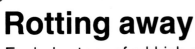

Each day tons of rubbish are tipped out at landfills, crushed into layers and buried. Some of it rots away.

This truck tips up its box to let rubbish fall out.

A machine called a toothed-wheel compactor presses rubbish into layers.

These heavy wheels and spikes help to flatten the rubbish.

Rotting food

Vegetable and garden waste rots into a rich muck called compost.

Many people make their own compost to help things grow. It is also made at a few special waste centres which sort food waste with machines.

The rubbish is covered with soil at the end of each day to keep litter and smells in and seagulls, rats and flies out.

This shovel scoops up and spreads the rubbish.

Some landfills are made in old quarries which are no longer used.

8

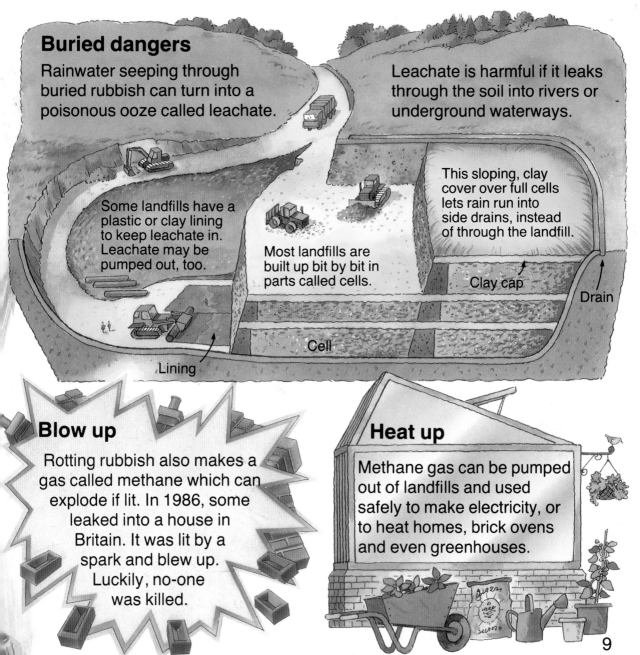

Buried dangers

Rainwater seeping through buried rubbish can turn into a poisonous ooze called leachate.

Leachate is harmful if it leaks through the soil into rivers or underground waterways.

Some landfills have a plastic or clay lining to keep leachate in. Leachate may be pumped out, too.

This sloping, clay cover over full cells lets rain run into side drains, instead of through the landfill.

Most landfills are built up bit by bit in parts called cells.

Clay cap

Drain

Lining

Cell

Blow up

Rotting rubbish also makes a gas called methane which can explode if lit. In 1986, some leaked into a house in Britain. It was lit by a spark and blew up. Luckily, no-one was killed.

Heat up

Methane gas can be pumped out of landfills and used safely to make electricity, or to heat homes, brick ovens and even greenhouses.

9

Up in flames

In big cities, rubbish may be burned in a place called an incinerator. This saves space in landfills, but gives off harmful gases, too.

1 Down the pit

Rubbish trucks tip rubbish straight into a deep pit at the incinerator.

3 Burning up

The furnace must be terribly hot to make sure the rubbish burns properly and gives off fewer harmful gases.

A person in a control room works the crane.

This grab crane moves along beams and lifts up and down.

2 Into the furnace

A crane grabs rubbish out of the pit and drops it down a chute into a giant oven called a furnace.

Hot air, gas and smoke go this way.

Furnace

Air is blown over and under the rubbish to make it burn well.

Ash goes this way.

This sloping floor is called a grate. Moving rollers on top carry the burning rubbish along.

These rollers turn and break up the rubbish to make it turn better.

10

4 Hot air

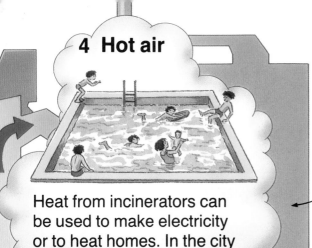

Heat from incinerators can be used to make electricity or to heat homes. In the city of Yokohama in Japan, it is used to heat swimming pools.

6 Dirty smoke

There are laws to make sure harmful smoke and gases are made cleaner, but some may still escape from the chimney.

Gases may be cleaned in tanks like this, with a chemical called lime.

Tanks like this collect dust and soot on big, metal plates or long tubes of cloth.

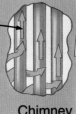

Chimney

5 Cool ashes

The ash is cooled in water and put on a moving belt. A magnet may be used to pick out some metal things which did not burn.

Water

Magnet

Ashes go to landfills.

Metal is crunched into blocks, sold for scrap and used again.

Out at sea

Some chemical waste used to be burned at sea in ships. Most countries have now stopped this as the waste gases were not always cleaned properly.

Down the drain

Each time you take a bath or flush the toilet, the waste water runs down the drainpipe to underground pipes called sewers. These take it to a place called a sewage works.

Sewage works are very important because they help to keep rivers clean and healthy.

This bend is always full of water to stop smells from coming back up.

Drainpipes

Rainwater often runs down drains into sewers.

Inside pipes take waste to drainpipes outside.

Waste in sewers is called sewage.

Sewers from homes join bigger ones under the street. These join giant sewers which go to the sewage works.

Sewers run downhill if possible. Sewage is pumped along uphill pipes.

By the sea

In some seaside towns, sewage pours out of a long sewer pipe into the sea. It may be cleaned a little first, but often it is not.

This raw sewage can make the sea horrid to swim in.

In the country

In some homes in the country, sewage goes to underground tanks. Every year or so it is pumped out by a tanker and taken to a sewage works.

This is called a septic tank.

These pipes let some liquid drain slowly into the soil.

At the sewage works

Sewage flows through many tanks at the sewage works. These take out different things to make it cleaner.

1 This screen traps wood, rags and other large things.

2 Grit sinks to the bottom of this tank and is pumped out.

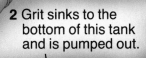

3 The sludgy part sinks down in this tank. From here sewage water and sludge go to different tanks.

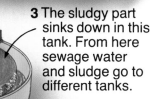

4 Sewage water goes here where it is mixed with a special liquid.

This liquid has lots of tiny, living things called bacteria in it.

These feed on dirt on the water to help to clean it.

Sewage water

Sewage sludge

6 Sewage sludge goes here where bacteria in the sludge turn some of the dirt into methane gas. This gas can be used to run the works.

5 The special liquid is pumped out of this tank and used again. The water goes into rivers.

7 The thickest sludge sinks down here, leaving water on top.

It is spread on land, burned or dumped at sea. Some countries have now stopped dumping it at sea.

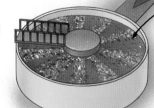

Dangerous waste

Waste which poisons water, soil or air is called pollution. There are laws to stop people from causing pollution, or to make them pay to have it cleaned.

In the rivers

Waste from sewage works and farms can pollute rivers with chemicals called phosphates and nitrates.

Phosphates come from sewage and cleaning liquids and powders.

Nitrates are added to land to help things grow. Some wash into rivers.

These chemicals help to make too many plants called algae grow.

Algae use up air and light needed by other plants and animals.

In the sea

Oil tankers can pollute seas if they leak, or if they break the law and wash out their tanks at sea.

Oil clogs up birds' wings and chokes fish.

Oil spills are expensive and difficult to clean.

This nuclear power station uses nuclear power to make electricity.

Below ground

Some waste from nuclear power stations can be dangerous for thousands of years. It must be looked after very carefully.

Some nuclear waste is set in concrete and sealed in drums and boxes. These will one day be stored deep underground.

Acid rain

Waste gases from cars, factories and power stations pollute the air and some can turn rain sour, or acid. More gases could be cleaned before leaving chimneys.

Acid rain poisons trees and lakes.

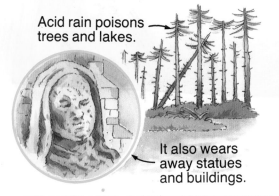

It also wears away statues and buildings.

Greenhouse gases

Some waste gases trap heat in the air like the glass of a greenhouse. This could warm up the Earth, causing parts of it to dry up. People need to stop making so many of these gases.

Heat escaping into space.

Heat from the sun.

Heat trapped by greenhouse gases.

Greenhouse gases build up in the air above Earth.

Car fumes

Car fumes make a poisonous, chemical smog when the sun shines on them. They also send out lead, which is harmful to breathe.

A filter called a catalytic converter can be fitted in car exhausts to clean gases which make smog and acid rain.

Drivers can use petrol without any lead in it.

The ozone layer

The ozone layer is a layer of gas around Earth which protects living things from harmful sunrays. Gases called CFCs break down this layer.

Some CFCs are used in refrigerators. Most countries have agreed to stop using all CFCs by the year 2000.

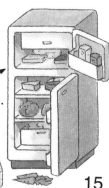

15

Using things again

Using rubbish again is called recycling. This saves using up so many things from the ground, called raw materials, to make new things. Some of these raw materials will one day run out.

Here are some things you can save which can be recycled, or used again.

Lots of this rubbish has been used to wrap or pack things. Using less packaging would make less rubbish.

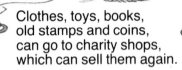

Clothes, toys, books, old stamps and coins, can go to charity shops, which can sell them again.

Food and garden waste can be turned into compost.

No waste

In Cairo, the capital city of Egypt, rubbish is collected by a group of people called the Zabaleens.

This rubbish will be sorted and sold to people who can use it again.

Paper, bottles, cans and rags can be made into new things. Plastic can also be recycled in this way.

Using things such as jars and bags again and again, is by far the best way of saving raw materials.

Paper chain

Saved waste paper and cardboard goes to a paper merchant's yard. Here it is sorted, pressed into bales and sent to a paper mill for recycling.

At the mill the paper is soaked in tanks of hot water and whisked into a mush called stock.

Make your own paper

Try recycling your own paper. It will help to show you what happens to paper at a paper mill.

Soak torn bits of newspaper overnight in a little water. Mash it with a fork.

Drain it. Roll it with a rolling pin and let it dry.

Trim the edges and paint it. You could use your paper as a table mat.

A machine spreads the stock onto a moving wire mesh to make paper.

The paper is fed onto a band of felt, which moves around different rollers.

As the stock drains, tiny thread-like fibres join up to make a big, sheet of paper.

Pumps underneath suck water out.

Heavy rollers squeeze water out of the paper.

Hot rollers dry it.

Polished rollers smooth it.

This roller winds it into a reel.

Boxes

Tissues

Recycled cardboard and paper go to factories to make some of these things.

Newspapers

More things to save

Recycling also saves energy. Energy comes from burning fuels such as oil. It takes much less energy to recycle things such as cans and bottles than it takes to make new ones from scratch.

Sorting cans

Cans are made from different metals which can be melted down and used again. Use a magnet to see which metal yours are made from.

Hold the magnet to the side.

Most cans are made from steel which sticks.

Steel cans are picked out at some transfer stations with giant magnets.

Many drinks cans are made from aluminium which does not stick.

Recycling aluminium cans saves almost all the energy it takes to make new ones.

Less pollution

Recycling also cuts down on pollution from incinerators, landfills and mines, as less rubbish is burned or buried and fewer raw materials are dug up. This makes the countryside look nicer, too.

Saving bottles

Any old jars and bottles you save for recycling can be melted down with these other things at a glass factory, to make new ones

Limestone

Soda-ash

Sand

Old glass can make up to half the amount. Using this much saves the most energy.

Sorting rubbish

Rubbish can be collected for recycling in different ways. In many places, you can take your old newspapers, bottles and cans to special bins in the street, called banks.

Bottle banks

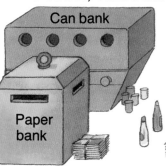

Can bank

Paper bank

Money back

In some places people pay a bit more for bottled goods in shops. They get this money back when they return the empty bottles.

A few banks take plastic bottles, too.

Some countries also have machines which give a coin for each aluminium can put in.

Sorting at home

In some places, people sort their rubbish into different bins or bags at home, to be collected separately.

In parts of Germany food scraps are put into one bin and collected separately to make compost.

Sorting centres

In a few countries, jumbled-up rubbish may be taken to a special waste centre to be shredded and pressed into pellets.

These pellets are burned in factories as a fuel.

Big things

Sometimes people need to get rid of things which are too big to go in the bin. They may be able to have them collected on special days, or they may take them to a recycling centre.

These centres have huge, metal crates for people to put things in. Many have recycling banks, too.

This crate is for garden waste.

Battery bank

Worn clothes and rags can be made into new things such as blankets.

Rag bank

Metal things may be put in a separate crate and sold to a metal merchant for recycling.

This tank collects old car oil to clean and use again. Pouring oil down drains or on the ground is not allowed, as it can seep into rivers.

Batteries have harmful acids in them which can leak. They can be recycled, but not many places do this yet.

Oil bank

Fly-tips

Dumping rubbish in places where it should not be is called fly-tipping. This spoils the towns and countryside.

Full crates are collected by trucks. Anything that cannot be recycled goes to a landfill.

Some rubble from building sites gets fly-tipped, even though this is not allowed.

On the scrap heap

Many old cars end up in a scrapyard. Here they are taken apart and crushed by powerful machines.

Trains and planes

Scrap steel from old bridges, ships, trains and planes is also melted down to make more things.

Useful things, such as engines, may be taken out and sold as spare parts.

The squashed cars go to a big scrap yard to be shredded into tiny bits of steel. These bits are melted down at a steel works.

This crane lifts the cars into a machine which flattens them.

Old batteries

The plastic cases and lead metal plates from car batteries can be recycled, too.

Used tyres

Tyres are difficult to bury or burn. People are always trying to find more ways to recycle them.

In the past

For thousands of years most people lived in small, farming villages. They did not have as much as many people have now and they wasted very little.

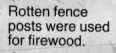
Rotten fence posts were used for firewood.

Food scraps were fed to animals.

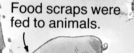
Food waste, ash, animal manure and sewage may also have been used to make compost.

Broken tools and clothes were mended.

Toilets in the past

Some castles had tiny rooms in the walls with a hole for a toilet. The waste fell down a chute into the moat or a pit.

These rooms are called garderobes.

About 500 years ago many people in towns used chamber pots, and tipped them out into the street below.

The first flush toilet was made in Britain in 1589 by Sir John Harington, but it was ages before most people had one.

Some rich people had really grand flush toilets.

Rubbish in the cities

About 200 years ago many cities got crowded and dirty as lots of people went to work in the new factories which were being built. Some people earned a tiny bit of money by getting rid of rubbish.

Dustmen were paid to collect rubbish from homes and clean roads.

Chimney sweep

Some children were made to scramble up inside chimneys with brushes to sweep away the soot.

Many poor people roamed the streets picking up rags, bones and scraps of metal or coal, to sell to others to use again.

Most waste was ash from fires. Some was sold to make bricks.

Crossing sweepers

Some people swept busy pavements and road crossings for the odd coin from passers-by.

Dog carts

About 100 years ago in Holland, dogs were used to pull dust carts.

23

Index

First published in 1991, Usborne Publishing Ltd, Usborne House, 83-85 Saffron Hill, London EC1N 8RT, England. Copyright © 1991 Usborne Publishing Ltd.